Forewo

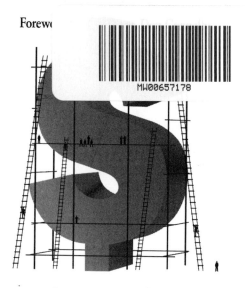

the ultimate
small CAP
business

Building A Financial Advisory Practice

Michael Roby

Disclaimer

This publication is designed to provide accurate and authoritative information in regard to starting and growing a financial advisory practice. It is sold with the understanding the publisher and author are not engaged in rendering legal, accounting, or investment advice, or attempting to provide a professional service to the reader in any way. If legal advice or other professional service is required, the services of a competent professional should be sought. In addition, there is no implied approval by any compliance or regulatory agency on any marketing or sales ideas. The publisher, author, and seller jointly and severally disclaim any warranty, express or implied, for any general or particular purpose, including business success and profitability, and any warranty of merchantability.

Internet addresses and telephone numbers given in this book were accurate at the time it went to press.

ISBN 13: 978-1-931945-86-8
ISBN 10: 1-931945-86-1

Library of Congress Catalog Number: 2008920227

Author photo by Thomas Strand Studio

Printed in the United States of America

First Printing: March 2008

12 11 10 09 08   5 4 3 2 1

Andover, Minnesota

Expert Publishing, Inc.
14314 Thrush Street NW,
Andover, MN 55304-3330
1-877-755-4966
www.expertpublishinginc.com

Dedication

I dedicate this book to those financial advisors that always keep their clients' best interests at heart, help their clients reach their financial objectives, and to those who have taught, managed, and inspired these advisors. In the business world there are no higher callings.

contents

foreword

by Don Connelly

If you are in sales, you better accept the fact that the size of your paycheck is 100 percent dependent upon your ability and your willingness to create and maintain long-term relationships.

Mike Roby knows that. And he also knows that a successful career in sales does not happen by accident.

Mike has thirty years' experience in sales and marketing and he is very, very good at what he does. He doesn't just tell you what to do. He tells you how to do it. Big difference!

A successful career in sales is a marathon, not a sprint. There are lots of lucky sprinters. There are no lucky marathon winners. Likewise, top sales people are not lucky. They have mastered the basics and they stick to them. Teaching the basics is what Mike is all about.

I cannot think of a time over the years when I have listened to Mike and not walked out of the room with an actionable "takeaway."

Let Mike teach you how to meet prospects on purpose, not by accident. That alone is worth the price of admission. And that's just the tip of the iceberg.

Don Connelly
Founder & CEO
Don Connelly & Associates LLC

preface

My journey in the financial services industry began in 1975 in Murray, KY. An older fraternity brother of mine chose to mentor me and suggested that I had an aptitude to be successful in the life insurance business and had what it took to be successful. With that proclamation, I thought I was a cinch to make it. So I began my career as a college agent for one of the best insurance sales companies in America.

However, after I had run through my good friends and family members, I was a wreck. I couldn't prospect. I was more concerned with being liked than being successful. To say I had call reluctance is a major understatement. I had (and still have) poor organizational skills. I "majored in minors." I could explain a ledger sheet, and I had the "One Card System" down pat, but I didn't sell much because I made a million excuses not to make calls.

My mentor (who eventually moved out of state to become a very successful general agent with the company) even arranged for me to be an intern at our home office. It was a wonderful experience. The company allowed me to work in their education and training division. I graded new agent training exams, helped develop new training programs, and had an opportunity to travel and showcase these materials. I learned a great deal, but after a six-month stint, I returned to Murray, and, once again, I froze at the thought of picking up the phone.

I thought I needed a change, so I changed companies after a year. (Sometimes advisors look for a geographic solution. Everything will be different with a change of scenery.) Not only did company number two hire me, they hired me as a *sales manager*. Go figure. I managed a sales unit of six salespeople. The youngest was eight years older than I was and the four oldest advisors' ages ranged from fifty-two to fifty-five. It was a recipe for disaster. After two years, I resigned the management position and became an agent in my old branch, and I proceeded to continue to fail for another six months. I decided to quit, but then I overheard my district manager tell someone he hoped that I would quit. I didn't want to fail, or leave because I was failing. However, I was failing and the failure had been all mine. I blamed it on circumstances, my managers, my family, and the economy. I refused to face the fact that I was the problem.

I was a failure in spite of having tremendous resources. However, I didn't want to be called a quitter and a failure. I still remember the booklet that spurred me on, *How I Went From Failure to Success in Selling,* by Elmer Hubbard. Hubbard stated his formula in very simple terms. He said, "Successful people are willing to do the things that failures won't do." I decided to become successful first, and *then* I would quit!

And that is exactly what I proceeded do. After several months, during which I worked hard and my sales soared, at a district meeting, it was announced that I was leading my district in sales, and later that day I resigned. A great firm with a different distribution model made me an offer. The person I would work for became one of the best mentors I ever had. I went from abject failure to some degrees of success, being named Rookie of the Year for the company, and, later, Account Executive of the Year. Over the next twenty years as a financial advisor, I had many wonderful teachers and experiences and some nice success. After over twenty years, I decided to become an investment wholesaler. My experience in the wholesaling business broadened my base of knowledge, as I have had the opportunity to learn from some of the *best* people in the financial services industry, as well as from some wonderful clients. My success came from persistence, learning from some great mentors, and developing a *system* for success as an advisor. You can develop your own system from the concepts discussed in this book. As you begin this process, a model for building or expanding your practice allows for more even growth. When building a model for a financial advisory practice, you can:

1. Build your own model,

2. Borrow a model from others, or

3. Create a combination of 1 and 2.

Success continues as a result of sticking to a workable, proven system. The Japanese have a concept called *kaizen*. We don't even have a word for it in English, but it means a never-ending improvement in products and processes. The Kaizen Institute describes *kaizen* as "designing and implementing processes that enable their organization to acquire the means for sustainability in performance and improvement." In America we have a saying that states, "If it ain't broke, don't fix it." But *kaizen* suggests that if it isn't broken, don't fix it; oil it, and continue to engineer and improve it.

This book is a reflection of my journey of over thirty years of experience in the distribution of financial service products as an entrepreneurial salesperson, trainer, and sales manager. My failures and successes, as well as the experiences of others, will provide you with workable, proven ideas to build your financial advisory business. Each section offers suggested Questions & Action Steps that will guide you through the process, and help you implement those ideas you find beneficial.

Enjoy the journey!

acknowledgments

Along the way I have had many people who taught, mentored, and encouraged me–the list might be longer than the text of the book, and many will be omitted as a result.

Ron Beshear stands out on the list, because he gave me my start in sales.

Other managers of note include Rick Lineberger, William Baird, and Joe Davis.

Dan Greenwell continues to be a coach and mentor.

Jack Walsh was tough, and still found ways to treat me like a son.

Keith Dayley's infectious enthusiasm and knowledge of his craft were a rare combination.

Doug Wood, Scott Logan, and Bob Cassato gave me the chance of a lifetime, and taught me how to take my professional skills to new levels.

There never was a better sales manager than Joe Harding. Joe is always teaching, coaching, and knows just what you need.

Mike Nicola trusted me to do my job, and behind the scenes was my advocate.

Jeff Duckworth is the consummate professional; any salesperson would do well to simply watch Jeff work.

Andy McFetridge is professional, multi-talented, and proof that nice guys finish first.

Jack Perry was a manager for whom I never had the pleasure of working, but he always went out the way to cheer me on.

Bill Montgomery took me under his wing and demonstrated what it meant to be a professional salesperson.

Don Connelly, the preeminent student and teacher of how to be a financial advisor, taught me sales concepts twenty years ago that I still use today, as he has to thousands of others. Over the last thirty-two years I have been to innumerable sales conferences and I have learned from all of them.

My customers and clients have truly been partners, and helped me to learn from my mistakes, and continue to do so.

I have been blessed to have tremendously talented people as part of my team. In three decades there have been many faces that have filled the roles, including executive assistants, office managers, marketing directors, service specialists, internal sales specialists, coaches, and research assistants. As someone who can be challenging to work with, I am amazed at the way they dedicated themselves to our purposes and the jobs at hand. Anything we accomplished would not have been possible without them.

The folks at Expert Publishing have helped me learn some of the finer nuances of writing, and I could only hope this work reflects their encouragement and wisdom. They continue the work of Dr. Jean Lorrah, Professor of English at Murray State University. Dr. Lorrah taught English Composition, and helped me discover that I could write.

Claudia Jenkins was a Murray State Graduate Assistant who taught Speech 101, and helped me discover the joy of public speaking.

"The Boys" (you know who you are) provide guidance, experience, and new ideas as we attempt to grow our businesses by providing more and more value to our speaking, consulting, and coaching clients.

John and Ramona Roby have been gone for many years. They raised five children and always had their kids' best interests at heart. In many ways, the oldest child is the toughest, and they worked hard as parents. They loved us unconditionally. I hope my work and my life honor them.

My children continue to inspire me, and give me purpose. They have learned that Dad is not perfect and is perfectly willing to admit he is still a work in progress, trying to learn something new every day. However, the grandchildren *think* I am perfect; I hope I don't disappoint them.

And my wife, Melanie, continues to prove I can sell, as my friends and those who know her consistently remind me that I "over-married" and by far received the better end of the deal. She always supports me, and she is my soul mate.

Last on this page but permeated throughout my life is Almighty God, who has blessed me beyond my wildest dreams in spite of my faults.

To these, and all the others who have touched my life, I will be eternally grateful.

chapter 1
Ultimate small CAP:
What You Need To Start

Owning your own business is part of the American dream. The ability to set your own hours, choose your clients, and unlimited income are all part of the dream. Whether you are an employee-advisor or an independent, you are in business for yourself. It is called, "You, Inc." To maximize the potential of your financial advisory practice, you *must* run it like a business—*your* business.

Challenges of Building a Business That Is Totally Dependent on You To Be Successful

Regardless of your distribution channel, you are running your own business. This applies to independent financial advisors, bank advisors, wirehouse brokers, and insurance agents. It does not matter if you are considered an employee or an independent contractor. Your success, or lack thereof, is 100 percent determined by you. Your attitude and activities determine your success. Your company, broker/dealer, management, and colleagues all play a part in the "Success Soup" that is your business; but in the end, you are the chef who determines if you succeed or not.

However, there are trade-offs. When you have your own business, long hours are involved. You (and your family) have to learn to live on a variable income. Clients are not always easy to deal with; they won't always be happy. Products and markets change, and you will have to make your peace with the fact that when you recommend financial products and services, there will be times when you (and your client) will not achieve the desired results. It will not necessarily be because you made a bad recommendation. Markets will sometimes turn against you, tax laws will change, clients will not have given you all of the information you need to make the best recommendation, or you may just be wrong. Sometimes your recommendations just will not work out. That is why we call it a financial advisory practice. (Doctors practice medicine, and attorneys practice law. In other words, doctors lose patients and attorneys lose trials, no matter how good they are. What they do is practice their profession.) So accept the fact that sometimes you will recommend products and services for clients that will not meet their needs nor solve their problems.

There are other considerations, as well. You may have to provide your own employee benefits, pay rent, and buy office furniture, equipment, computers, and supplies. You must manage your time; have enough self-discipline to know when it is time to go to work and when you should go home. When you are paid on commissions or fees, there is never a paid vacation.

Michael Gerber, founder of E-Myth Worldwide says, "Within any given year, close to one million people start a small business in the U.S. Sadly, at least 40 percent of those businesses fail within the first year. The failure rate over time is nothing short of staggering. Of the one million U.S. small businesses started this year, more than 800,000 (80 percent) of them will be out of business within five years and 96 percent will have closed their doors before their tenth birthday." While these are daunting statistics, they reflect the experience of the masses. They do *not* predict the future for a particular individual; they have nothing to do with *you* and *your success*.

There is a restaurant on the north side of St. Paul, MN, that has a sign in their entrance that says,

> *"The Only Thing More Overrated Than Natural Childbirth Is Owning Your Own Business."*

Hmmm—I wonder why I eat there.

In other words, while running a financial advisory practice is not easy, it can be tremendously rewarding. Advisors provide economic and lifestyle security to families and businesses. They can help their clients make decisions that will provide money when they need it most. Advisors help people retire with dignity, educate their children and grandchildren, and protect themselves, their families, and their businesses against unexpected contingencies. Our business, when practiced properly, is a noble calling.

What is Ultimate Small Cap (USmC)?

The size of a company is measured by something called market capitalization. Market capitalization ("Cap" for short) represents the aggregate value of a company or stock. Companies are often categorized as large, mid, or small cap. If you choose, or have chosen to be financial advisor, I believe you have the Ultimate Small Cap Company. Let's compare the concept of Ultimate Small Cap with the opportunity to owning a McDonald's™ Franchise. McDonald's is arguably the best and certainly the largest fast food franchise in the world, as measured by size, number of stores, and success probabilities for new franchisees.

However, it can also be argued successfully that the reason for their success is because they have the best hamburgers. What one must realize is that McDonald's[1] doesn't sell hamburgers; it sells a business system. While this business system has been phenomenally successful, it isn't inexpensive. What you pay for in purchasing the McDonald's business system is the accumulated knowledge from over fifty years[2] of experience servicing over 30,000 restaurants worldwide.

One can get into the business by purchasing an existing restaurant (subject to approval by McDonald's Corp.) or by starting a new store. The initial down payment can range from 25 percent to 40 percent, depending on whether you are purchasing an existing store or buying a new franchise. In terms of cash required, McDonald's requires that a *minimum* of $250,000[3] of the down payment be from non-borrowed resources—they want the new franchisee to have some skin in the game— and McDonald's strongly encourages prospective franchisees to have an even larger portion of the down payment and/or purchase price come from personal funds. Debt service must be paid back over seven years, and McDonald's does not provide financing, although they state that McDonald's franchisees typically receive favorable terms.

In addition to purchasing the franchise (which does not include real estate costs) a franchisee must pay service fees based upon the restaurant's performance.

1   Information in this section is taken from www.McDonald's.com.
2   McDonald's Corp. was founded by Ray Kroc on April 15, 1955.
3   McDonald's will accept some negotiable securities as a portion of the down payment.

These fees are currently in the neighborhood of 4 percent of monthly sales. It is difficult to criticize the McDonald's franchise system, but it requires a huge front end financial commitment, in addition to perpetual monthly service fees. So how does this contrast with the opportunity provided for those who choose to be financial advisors?

While building a financial advisory business requires relatively little *capital* investment, it *does* require sacrifice and hard work, also referred to as sweat equity. You *will* have to invest capital—money into your business at different intervals; however, you can't spend your way into prosperity. Brent Thompson, former president of Trigg County Farmers Bank in Cadiz, KY, once told me, "You have to spend money to make money, but you have to have money to spend money!" However, the capital investment required to start a financial advisory practice is relatively small considering the income and wealth building potential.

Depending on your distribution channel, you may be required to have some source of supplementary income while you build your financial advisory cash flow, and possibly, working capital, while you get your business started. Even if you are working as an employee, you must look at entering the financial advisory business as if you are an entrepreneur; it will take time to get your business ramped up. You must be willing to work like very few people are willing to work to get your business started. If you do, you will be able to live like few can afford to live and be able to live that way for the rest of your life.

How You And Your TEAM™ Can Use This Book

If you are in the early stages of building your business, you are a one-person show. If you have been in practice for some time, you will have a staff. To maximize the potential of your business, though, your staff must be a TEAM.

A TEAM is:

> T   = Trained
> E   = Enthusiastic
> A   = Assistants who are
> M   = Managed by *you*

No matter what stage you are in your journey, there is information here that you, and your TEAM can use to help you build your business. My hope is that you will make *quantum* changes in your vision for the future by implementing *incremental* changes in activities, methods, and systems.

A To Do section is in the back of the book for you to make notes of ideas you wish to implement. If you are new to the business, this book provides a comprehensive overview of all of the elements of building a successful financial advisory business. If you are an experienced advisor, the objective is not to totally change the way you do business, but rather, to *refine* the way you do business.

IMPORTANT NOTE:

As an additional benefit of purchasing this book, you are entitled to complimentary additional sales resources at www.michaelroby.com/usc. Use the word "Extra" as your password.

What This Book Won't Do

This book is designed to help you greatly increase your chances of success if you are starting to build your business, or help you increase the quantity and quality of your business if you are already successful. This book ***will not*** make you successful, and it certainly won't save an advisor from failing. What you will find are many ideas, strategies, tools, and techniques that are proven. Take what you like, and leave the rest.

Questions & Action Steps

- *If you are new to the business, what do you want this book to do for you?*

- *If you are an experienced advisor, what would you like to change about your business, and what do you want to learn from this book?*

Go to www.michaelroby.com for a Goals Worksheet.

chapter 2

Ultimate small CAP:
Your Financial Advisory Business

One of your first considerations is to decide what type of business you are building. There are two basic structures for an advisory business, but each has several variations:

- Single Advisor Practice
- Multiple Advisor Practice

Each structure has advantages and disadvantages, and your choice will be based upon your personal preferences in having to deal with colleagues and your long-term objectives for disposition of the business.

Single Advisor Practice

This structure typically features you as the advisor with an assistant or multiple assistants. The advantages include the ability to convene decision-making sessions quickly; you can always have a conversation with the boss. While, over time, you will rely heavily on staff to participate in the decision-making process, the buck stops with you. This requires that you be consistently effective at managing *all* aspects of the business. As your business grows, you will delegate or outsource in the area of non-revenue producing activities. It is easier to maintain your focus on your professional objectives, and keeping score requires but a few basic metrics of success.

The challenges include not having colleagues to act as a day-to-day sounding board, and the ultimate sale of your practice may be more difficult to negotiate, because *you* are the business. Of course, a price tag can be put on recurring fee income and trail commissions, but the business's brand and the goodwill of the business are *you*. This makes valuing the practice a mere function of determining the present value of the future income; but without you there to continue to nurture and maintain your key client relationships the business has greater value.

Multiple Advisor Practice

This structure is developed through acquiring partners or recruiting associate advisors. The advantage of a Multiple Advisor Practice (MAP) is the built-in market for a practice when an advisor decides to retire, as well as for succession planning in the event of death or disability. A MAP also creates greater net worth due to the goodwill represented by multiple clienteles. When you have a MAP, you generate an inherent sense of continuity that lends itself to perpetuation of the practice, and clients love continuity. However, there are significant differences in building a MAP with partnerships versus recruiting advisors to work in your business.

Partnerships[1]

Finding and maintaining synergistic partner relationships can be a challenge. Partnerships can be like marriages; the bliss of dating is much different from the day-to-day work of maintaining the relationship. Like marriage, if it just doesn't work out as you expected, it might end up in court.

Successful partnerships require compatibility and likeability, but also complementary skill sets. Without all three, the partnership may experience periods of extreme stress, which can result in turmoil, which can lead to dissolution. When considering a partnership, ask yourself the following questions:

* *What can I do to help [Blank] enhance his/her business?*

* *What can [Blank] do to help me succeed in my business?*

---

1   For this discussion, the term "Partnership" includes formal partnerships, informal joint-office associations, LLC's, and the various forms of incorporation.

- *How do we complement each other?*
- *In what ways will we potentially clash?*

Often partners neglect to take the formal legal steps that address dissolution contingencies. Many advisors do not practice what they preach. Good planning dictates that advisors make certain that they seek legal and tax counsel from legal and accounting advisors that are experienced in business structure.[2] By seeking counsel when forming a partnership, or other legal business entity, you reduce the possibility of problems in the future.

Recruiting Advisors

Using recruiting to build a MAP is an entirely different process. So often advisors who choose to build their business by recruiting forget that they must also continue building their personal practice and maintaining their client service standards. Don't fall in the trap of thinking, "I make money off the efforts of others!" Building a MAP with recruiting builds the value of the business by creating a sales force that has value at the time of sale. You should always plan for, and depend on, your personal practice to meet your personal income needs. In fact, you will *spend* money in the early stages of building through recruiting, in addition to expending additional sweat equity.

---

2   Don't be guilty of what so many of your clients are guilty of doing-procrastinating and/or trying to skate through on your own, without a competent advisor.

Recruiting is a three-step process:

* *Attracting* the right candidate
* *Training* for success
* *Retaining* valuable TEAM members

Attracting potential advisors requires having a sales presentation, as does *any* sale. You need to build a recruiting presentation that answers the following questions in the potential advisor's mind.

* *Is this opportunity the right fit for me?*
* *Is this a business I want to join?*
* *What does this business offer that will help me build and grow MY business?*
* *What's in it for me?*

Training requires a slightly different set of skills than those utilized when working with clients. Selling requires educating a prospect by describing benefits supported by features, and leading them to take action. Training provides usable information that can be applied to certain situations. Selling is "let's do this today," while training is "take this and use it." Many advisors that recruit additional advisors neglect to provide training opportunities on the basis that "they are building their own business; they have to find their own way." While this is true, you must face the fact that some training is required, because if the new advisor could become successful totally on their own, *why did they join you in the first place?*

Experienced advisors require different training from the training you would provide to new advisors. Experienced advisors need to know process, as well as skill-set improvement, while new advisors need basic sales training *and* process. Regardless of the experience level you decide to recruit, you MUST have a training plan in place *before* you contract with a new recruit to your business. Consider purchasing one of the excellent training programs available, and supplement that training with your own processes and procedures education. In time, you may wish to build a proprietary training program, however.

Retaining advisors, like every aspect of our business, contains elements of art *and* science. Advisors want, need, and deserve a collegial environment in which they can grow their business. Synergistic training and educational opportunities provide an atmosphere that is conducive to helping them grow and develop their business. The leader of the group establishes a team-consciousness and esprit de corps; leadership makes the difference.

Mission Statement

Much has been written about mission statements. (Googling "mission statements" results in 21,200,000 hits.) Suffice it to say that it makes sense to have a sense of mission, a sense of purpose. In order to have a mission statement that works, build in answers to the following questions:

- What is the clientele you seek to serve?
- What outcomes do you hope to achieve for your clients?
- What will be the core products and services you will offer?
- What are your core beliefs and values?

Notice this format omits what is in it for you. A mission statement is not the place to list *your* goals. However, you will need to overlay your mission statement over your business plan to make certain they are congruent.

 Questions & Action Steps

- *If you are an established advisor, and you want to expand your business, what method do you prefer—a Partnership (where you associate with a person or persons who will be your peers), or Recruiting (where you hire and train associates), and why?*

- *If you are already in a partnership, what has helped make it successful?*

- *If you are already in a partnership, what would improve the relationship and the business?*

- *Do you have a mission statement? Does it accurately reflect your values and will it help you attain your personal goals? If not, write a new mission statement using the format discussed in this chapter. Also look at other resources to help you write a mission statement that works for you.*

chapter 3
Ultimate small CAP:
Business Objectives

You chose to be a financial advisor. If Bill Gates (pretty smart guy) needed a business plan to build Microsoft, a business plan is an essential tool to help you realize your goals and objectives.

The first step in this section of your business planning is to define your objectives in specific terms. Consider addressing goals such as:

- Gross commissions
- Number of clients
- Professional designations acquired

Set goals for each year for five years. Rely on the opinions of your mentors, managers, and other colleagues. Set goals without regard for *how* you will achieve those goals. Set your goals and then proceed to determine how you will achieve them.

Existing advisors, in all likelihood, have an existing business plan. Many business planning templates exist with a range of sometimes complex planning steps. Take a look at the following template, which has been proven to be not only simple but effective:

- Keep what you have
- Get all of their business
- Find more like them

Keep What You Have

Keep what you have refers to keeping your existing clients and relationships. According to business retention coach Vadim Kotelnikov:

1. Acquiring new customers can cost five times more than satisfying and retaining current customers.

2. A 2 percent increase in customer retention has the same effect on profits as cutting costs by 10 percent.

3. The average company loses 10 percent of its customers each year.

4. A 5 percent reduction in customer defection rate can increase profits by 25-125 percent, depending on the industry.

5. The customer profitability rate tends to increase over the life of a retained customer.

Many advisors constantly look for the next big thing, or can't-miss direct mail piece, the next seminar that prospects will flock to in droves. At the same time, they neglect their clients. If, in fact, it is five to seven times harder to get a new client than to keep an existing client, seriously consider what you can *do* to keep your existing clients. In spite of these facts, many experienced advisors continue to chase new blood for their business.

What we should do is structure our business to cater to the needs and desires of our existing clients *first* and then prospect for new clients. If you are new to the business, and have no clients to keep, you should focus some attention on maintaining existing relationships that can become centers of influence.

In building your business plan, devote a section to defining how you want your clients to view you and your services. In the book, *7 Habits of Highly Effective People*, Dr. Stephen Covey suggests that we "write the last chapter first." In other words, define *precisely* what you want your clients' experience of working with you to be, not from *your* perspective, but from *their* perspective.

Get All of Their Business

A ticking time bomb lurks in many practices today that will explode for many advisors, and leave them, their businesses, and their finances destroyed. This explosion will be the direct result of practitioners positioning themselves as "Financial Planners" when the vast majority of their business is devoted to one area of practice, such as Risk Management, Investment Management, Asset Allocation, or Tax Planning.

If you hold yourself out as a "Financial Planner," or a "Financial Advisor," you should address *all* of these planning areas. By addressing each of these areas in a comprehensive manner, advisors not only meet their clients' needs better, but generate more revenue.

Please note that you cannot be all things to all clients, but you can draw upon other resources to meet all of your clients' financial needs. While it makes sense to specialize, you don't want to leave your clients exposed to risk, and you don't want to leave money on the table.

Find More Like Them

This represents the prospecting piece. To be successful long term requires a new client acquisition strategy. The strongest practices employ creative, professional referral generation strategies, procedures, and technologies to expand their client base. When you truly create a strong and unique client experience, you stand in a very solid position to ask for and expect referrals. A word of caution: you don't want to appear needy or desperate for referrals. This point emphasizes the need for professional referral/or introduction generation technologies.

In the coming chapters, I will discuss specific techniques and strategies to achieve these objectives.

Questions & Action Steps

Complete questions one and two as you think your clients might answer them. Answer the remaining questions from your perspective.

1. *The reasons I have continued to retain [Advisor] are because…*

2. *The biggest thing [Advisor] could do better is [Blank].*

3. *How effective am I at retaining my clients? Why or why not?*

4. *What percentage of my clients have financial product relationships with someone in addition to me? Why might that be so? Might I be able to capture more of their business, and what effect would it have on my practice?*

5. *What percentage of my clients refer me to others each year?*

For Referral/Introduction Resources, go to
www.michaelroby.com/usc

chapter 4
Ultimate small CAP:
Sales And Marketing

As children, we all played with building blocks. If you wanted to build high, you had to have a good foundation. Strong financial advisory businesses rest on several foundational components. These activity-based components must be performed reasonably well on a consistent basis to see your business grow to its potential.

These eight components form the basis for the USmC Business Plan. There is no end to the number of business planning templates designed for financial advisors. The template offered in this book is but one of many, but its beauty is in its simplicity. The USmC Basic Business Building Blocks are:

- Sales (covered in this chapter)
- Marketing (covered in this chapter)

- Client service (covered in this chapter)
- Administration (see chapter 5)
- Education and training (see chapter 6)
- Practice management (see chapter 6)
- Administrative staffing—Building a TEAM (see chapter 6)
- Recruiting (If you choose to build a multiple advisor practice—see chapter 2)

Sales

Sometimes we forget we are salespeople. We can be the best organizers; we can design the best portfolios, provide exceptional service, complete our paperwork completely, and know every stock symbol for every issue on the exchange. However, if we can't present persuasively, answer objections effectively, and professionally convince our clients to take action, none of our other activities matter. We can't truly serve people unless we can persuade them to adopt our recommendations. The most effective salespeople have the following characteristics.

- Client centered
- Strong work ethic
- Sincere interest in others
- Trustworthy

- Focused on their clients' goals *first*
- People oriented
- Self-disciplined

When a person has these characteristics, he/she has the ability to be successful as an advisor, but these characteristics are, to some extent, innate. This is the source of the term, "born salesperson." Salespeople are not born, and an individual can have these characteristics and still not be able to sell. The missing ingredient is sales skills. Sales skills are taught; they are not a part of your DNA. Sales skills can be broken down into skill sets as follows:

- Approach
- Warm up
- Fact-finding/listening
- Presentation
- Answering objections
- Closing
- Service after the sale

If you feel you are lacking in any of these areas, there are innumerable resources for each of the skill sets. One of the best repositories of sales training resources is Nightengale-Conant, which is one of the, if not the, largest distributor of sales and personal development training tools in the world. Their roots go back to the 1950s and two legendary figures in selling: Earl Nightengale and Lloyd Conant. No matter what area of personal development you would like to improve, you can find it at

www.nightengale.com

 Questions & Action Steps

1. *What areas of sales technique could I improve?*

2. *What resources will I access to make the needed improvements in my sales technique?*

Develop Your Unique Sales Process

Beyond basic sales skills, you develop a unique sales process. This is commonly referred to as your style of selling. For beginners, start with the basics and seek out the best training you can find; you will develop your own style in time. Before you get too carried away with thinking, "I don't want to use a prepared or canned presentation," deliver the presentation taught to you until you prove you can use it successfully. After you have learned the basics, then you can make your presentations your own.

For seasoned advisors, you have already developed your style. It is often helpful for those with experience to catalog their style. In other words, diagram your unique selling process on paper. Process means there is a definable order in the way you begin an interview, gather information, process that information, formulate recommendations, and ask the client for the order.

Why is this helpful? By knowing precisely what your process looks like, you can fine tune every section of the presentation, with the result being improved closing ratios and increased sales. A slight improvement in technique translates to an even greater sales increase *without working harder, more sales calls, or more prospects.* Review your sales proficiency and effectiveness and consider where you might be able to improve.

A final word for the novice or new advisor; there are only two ways you can increase sales:

* Technique
* Activity

Technique takes time. Activity can be increased immediately!

Develop Your Unique Sales Metrics

Jack Walsh, founder of Money Concepts International, said many years ago, "You can't manage what you can't measure." Jack was always years ahead of his time, but he was also very basic in his approach to the business. The professional knows you must keep score. By tracking activities, you can determine very easily the effectiveness of your sales process, as well as where you need to improve. Brad Connors, of Waseca, MN, keeps track of the time he spends fact-finding, presenting, doing client reviews, case preparation, and presentations. Comparing this information to his sales results allows him to adjust his activity to meet his business and personal goals. Over a period of years, Brad has developed an ability to make significant increases in his business by making adjustments to his process and presentations as well.

Other Sales Resources

Home office field sales specialists and product whole-salers provide excellent sales training resources. Utilize these specialists, and be loyal to those who supply ideas that help you improve your sales skills.

Sales conferences provide education, tools, techniques, and inspiration to become a better salesperson. Most companies provide different training conferences and opportunities, but you can find exceptional material in independent conferences.

There is a growing movement towards sales coaches. A sales coach, like a speech coach or a personal athletic trainer, can help you improve your performance by providing one-on-one sales training and guidance.

Trade organizations, such as the National Association of Insurance and Financial Advisors (NAIFA), Financial Planning Association (FPA), American College, and College for Financial Planning offer basic, as well as advanced, training symposiums in addition to periodic local gatherings. The mark of professionals is that they will associate and collaborate with the colleagues and competitors for the betterment of themselves and their industry.

Questions & Action Steps

1. *If a client or colleague were to ask, "Tell me about your process," how would you describe your process to him/her? How would you do it in three sentences, or fewer?*

2. *What is your present level of sales activity, measured by fact-finding, presenting, doing client reviews, case preparation, and presentations? Is this level adequate to help you meet your objectives?*

3. *What resources can you utilize to improve your sales communication skills?*

For information on sales coaching, go to www.michaelroby.com/coaching

Marketing

Advisors often confuse sales and marketing. Selling is only a part of marketing. Sales is the knee-to-knee interaction with clients and prospects that (hopefully) produces business. The American Marketing Association defines marketing as "an organizational function and a set of processes for creating, communicating, and delivering value to customers and for managing customer relationships in ways that benefit the organization and its stakeholders." Marketing also includes promotion, positioning, and branding.

American history gives us a relevant analogy. By the time the American pioneers reached the Great Plains, they were skilled farmers. If they arrived on a choice piece of prairie in early spring, established a homestead, put a crop in the ground, cultivated, and received the blessing of good weather, they could expect a crop in the fall. However, if they didn't hunt between early spring and the harvest in the fall, they would have starved.

Selling is hunting. Marketing is farming. My experience is that those who fail in this business do too much of one and not enough of the other.

Your Natural Market

Don't neglect your natural market. This is the area that you feel most comfortable. It will be defined by your income, age, previous occupation, life experiences, and social status. Start here first, or if you are experienced, don't neglect it.

Keith Daley of Jordan, UT, is a retired sales trainer, and one of the best who ever lived. His enthusiasm, experience, and concern for his students helped thousands of men and women become more effective sales professionals. Keith tells a story of how he became quite successful in life insurance sales at a very young age. His manager declared that he could do even more business if he would just prospect up. So Keith, at age twenty-four, started calling on the doctors, lawyers, and senior successful business people in his community. He failed miserably. These successful people, most all much older than Keith, couldn't accept financial advice from someone so young and inexperienced. After going back to his comfort zone, Keith recovered, and his sales went up. As he gained more experience, and more importantly, made more money, his social standing increased, and his comfort zone expanded with the growth of his circle of social contacts. At that point he was able to prospect among more affluent potential clients, because he was working in a circle in which he was now comfortable and accepted.

Market and prospect to your natural market first. Maintain old relationships and grow from there. No matter how much experience you have, examine your existing relationships for opportunities.

Building Brand

David McNally is one of the top authorities on branding in the world today. In *Be Your Own Brand*, which David co-authored with Karl D. Speak, they state, "Really great brands, whether personal or product, transcend the quantifiable to conjure up powerful emotions, especially positive emotions. When a business brand achieves that status, it has real power. And when a personal brand builds similar linkages to the heart as well as the head, it too has real power." Everyone has a brand; the question is did you design it or leave it to chance? Building brand is a process, but a process you can guide and tailor to meet your mission, values, and business objectives. McNally and Speak's book is an excellent resource to help guide you in the process of building your brand.

Multi-Tiered Marketing

This is a concept that says an advisor always has more than one marketing program in place. A Multi-Tiered Marketing Program allows an advisor to have several marketing campaigns running simultaneously. Successful execution involves:

1. Proper planning
2. Execution of these activities
3. Follow-up and review

This ensures a steady stream of prospects and appointment opportunities. Also, several ongoing campaigns diversify your marketing efforts, which prevent you from having slumps and dry spells.

Some examples of marketing programs include, but are not limited to:

- Direct mail
- Pre-approach mail campaigns
- Referred lead technologies
- Constant client contact
- Seminars
- Public speaking
- Advertising
- Newsletters
- Radio/Print market reports
- Writing articles for newspapers
- Teaching adult education
- Email campaigns and correspondence
- Networking groups
- Sponsorship of athletic teams or community groups

By running two to five marketing programs simultaneously, you can generate a significant number of sales opportunities.

Periodically examine[1] your marketing to review the sources of your sales. If one program appears to be more successful, *do more of it.* If a program does not provide meaningful sales activity, or foster you long-term relationships, *quit doing it* and replace it with another marketing strategy.

It is amazing that advisors will run a marketing campaign for extended periods of time without acceptable results. So to fix the problem, they *do more of the same thing*! (It has been said the definition of insanity is doing the same thing over and over and expecting different results.)

Questions & Action Steps

1. *What market programs have worked the best for you in the past?*

---

1   Give your programs a chance to be successful. Don't jump from one program to the next looking for instant success.

2. *If you had to pick three (3) marketing programs to run simultaneously, what would they be?*

3. *What marketing programs do you implement that do not produce good results? Why are you still using them?*

Client Service

Financial advisors provide and perform service. The products we sell are all commodities. Service stands as one of the key ingredients in our clients' experience of working with us. A solid long-term business requires a commitment to high quality service. Dynamic growth demands service that exceeds client expectations. It is not enough that, if surveyed, your clients say they are satisfied. In *Raving Fans*, by Kenneth Blanchard and Sheldon Bowles, they state "Your customers are only satisfied because their expectations are so low and because no one else is doing better. Just having satisfied customers isn't good enough anymore. If you really want a booming business, you have to create Raving Fans." However, in spite of what they tried to tell you in kindergarten, it is impossible to treat everyone the same. Give everyone excellent service, but give better clients *exceptional* service. How does the financial advisor determine how much service to deliver? An effective client service program (which also translates into increased sales) requires client classification and service standards.

Client Classification

The concept of client classification is certainly not a new concept. Traditionally, advisors classified clients as A, B, or C, and followed the Pareto Principle, also known as the 80/20 Rule. In 1906, economist Vilfredo Pareto, a native of Italy, created a mathematical formula to describe the unequal distribution of wealth in his country, observing that 20 percent of the people owned 80 percent of the wealth. Salespeople cater to the top 20 percent of their clients, which, in theory, produce 80 percent of the revenue to their business.

Most advisors classify clients based on feel, or gut. It makes sense to develop a simple methodology for client classification.

"A" clients will have many characteristics, but it is best to keep the process short. Three criteria make up the basis of any client classification system.

- Assets under management (with you or others)
- The ability and inclination to be a center of influence for you and your business
- Reasonable expectations of you as the advisor

A word of caution: to be an "A" client, they *must* have reasonable expectations. Life is too short.

Excellent versus Exceptional Service

Every client deserves excellent service. Some clients deserve *exceptional* service. My oldest son is a sales manager for a car dealership near Atlanta, GA. While visiting our home in Minnesota, he overheard a phone conversation I was having with an advisor, and I mentioned providing *some* clients with exceptional service. He exclaimed, "All of my customers get excellent service!"

I couldn't agree more. If you have only ten cents under management, or one $10,000 life insurance policy on the books for a client, that one client deserves *excellent* service. If you are privileged to be a client's advisor, and if you make one penny off a client's account, then you owe that client *excellent* service. Your best clients, however, deserve *exceptional* service. So definitions of these terms of service are in order.

Excellent service is defined as follows:

* Prompt execution and submission of all trades, orders, and applications

* Prompt return of all phone calls and written correspondence

* The offer of a periodic review

Exceptional service is anything above and beyond excellent service.

These definitions are simple and basic enough to stand on their own. An advisor establishes what exceptional service will be for his/her practice, and what entitles (yes, I said *entitles*) a client to exceptional service. You should provide enough significant value to your clients that it is a *privilege* for them to say you are their advisor and you provide them exceptional service.

Exceptional service can be quantified and defined in a number of ways. Client appreciation events, more frequent personal and written contacts, supplemental portfolio reports, additional educational and informational services, and client entertainment are just some of the ways you can provide exceptional service.

Client service standards allow you to establish definable levels of service for all of your clients. By establishing service standards, you achieve multiple objectives. Service standards allow you to provide quality service to your clients, provide a structure to your business that establishes client review frequencies, and automate the client service process for you and your staff. It can be helpful to an advisor to construct a visual example of service standards by building a service matrix. Here is an example of a service standard matrix, with the numbers in the matrix indicating the annual frequency of the client service activity.

	Personal Contacts	Reviews	Reviews In Person
"A" Clients	12	4	4
"B" Clients	4	2	1
"C" Clients	2	1	?

You may say that you have true "A" clients that not only don't need you to review their accounts four times each year, they don't *want* to have that many reviews. No problem. These standards are not what you actually execute for every client, but what you are willing to do if they want you to do so. In other words, if an "A" client wants you to sit down with them quarterly, you will be willing to do it. You (or a member of your team) calls the client monthly to offer a service, comment on their account, extend birthday or anniversary greetings, or just to check in with them.

Other examples of service delivery headings that you can build into the service matrix include:

- Newsletters
- Email blasts
- Mail articles
- Assistant calls
- Holiday/Greeting cards
- Anniversary cards
- Tickets to sporting, cultural, and entertainment events

In other words, *you* get to decide what you offer to your clients in the way of exceptional service.

Questions & Action Steps

1. *How have you classified clients in the past?*

2. *Does this system still work for you, or would it help your business to revise it? What other factors might you consider in classifying clients?*

Go to www.michaelroby.com/usc to download a
service matrix template

chapter 5
Ultimate small CAP:
Office Administration

As your business grows, it will create a larger volume of back-office work. Early in your career you literally wear more hats; in some cases you wear all of them. If you start getting behind the curve when it comes to office administration, your business efficiency will begin to deteriorate, and your sales effectiveness will drop. Office administration is the wrench that jams the gears of many successful practices.

Great advisors are technically competent to advise their clients, have exceptional people skills, and can sell. However, too many advisors never develop their teams, systems, and processes to maximize their personal effectiveness and streamline their business. An office works efficiently when you develop two essential components: processes and people.

Process Development

One challenge that advisors face is that they continually redevelop recurring processes. For example, when they want to send a letter to thank a new client, they always dictate a personal letter. Also, when a form needs to be sent to a client for a signature, they draft a short note to act as a cover letter. Never create the same thing twice. This concept applies to case preparation, business processing, client service, marketing, and client correspondence.[1] It is easy to personalize a form letter by adding a short paragraph of a personal nature, and that is much more efficient than rewriting the same document over and over.

Every broker/dealer (B/D) has a standard operating procedures manual governing conduct of a registered rep. Consider developing a Standard Operating Procedures Manual (SOPM) for your business. Of course, this does not supersede your Registered Representative's manual, but covers the routine activities that you and your team undertake as you build your business and service your clients. There are several reasons for building such a manual.

- Using the same process repeatedly insures quality and saves time.

- Communication with your team is enhanced, with fewer misunderstandings and mistakes.

---

1   Always comply with FINRA regulations, as well as those of your broker/dealer's compliance department.

- It becomes easier to deliver high quality service to your clients.

- Training new associates and staff takes less time.

- By having a set of established office procedures, you reduce the number of potential compliance problems in your business, as well as the potential for errors and omissions.

- If you ever choose to sell your business or bring on partners, having a set system adds greatly to the value of the business. (Remember, McDonald's does not sell hamburgers; they sell a business system.)

- You have more time to do what you get paid to do—work with clients.

How do you get started? Of course, you may not be able to pull a member of your team off of their daily, weekly, and monthly duties strictly to develop a SOPM, but any time you have a process that you repeat, make a brief outline of the process (or have the person that completes the process make an outline), including answers to the following questions.

- What is the objective of the process?

- What are the tasks that need to be accomplished to complete the objective?

- Which staff position is responsible?

- What are the time frames for completion?

- What reporting is needed, and what checks and balances are required?

Examples of the types of processes you will include in a Standard Operating Procedures Manual include:

- New business processing checklist
- Sample copies of forms that are used in the business
- Case preparation checklist
- Telephone answering procedures
- Seminar marketing procedures
- Procedures for ordering sales materials and office supplies
- Monthly client reviews
- Thank you letters and other routine correspondence

Anytime you write a letter or a memo, save the letter and build a catalog of these letters. If these letters are formatted so they can be integrated with the mail-merge feature of your database, you will save a tremendous amount of time over the years and keep your staff happy and productive, in addition to helping increase sales and providing enhanced client service.

This is not a project you will complete over a weekend, but rather is a continual work-in-progress. But started is better than not done. Every time you write a letter, complete paperwork, or execute a marketing/sales strategy, ask yourself, "Will I/we do this again for other prospects or clients in the future?" If the answer is yes, consider building a process for that activity.

Staff Development

Often advisors ignore staff development by thinking, "It is easier to do it myself." Advisors also excuse themselves from training their people because they don't want to manage people, they just want to work with their clients; all they want to have to do is sell. Besides, why can't people just do their jobs? Why can't they figure things out on their own?

Developing the people that work in your business *does* take time, but it *saves* time in the long run. If you lack experience training or managing a sales support team, a great place to turn is *The One Minute Manager*. If you have read it before, re-read it every one to two years. The beauty of this book is its simplicity. Another exceptional book for those managing people is *The One Minute Manager Meets the Monkey*. The "monkey" means the next move. By managing the monkeys/next moves in your business, you control your schedule and improve your effectiveness.

When you add administration staff, you create another challenge: getting and keeping everyone on the same page (even if it is only you and one assistant). Decide who has ownership of the component parts of the administration of the business. Just because one person has ownership (or responsibility—call it what you will), that doesn't mean that person will work in a vacuum. You will still discuss all areas of the business with your team, no matter how large it gets. However, if a person has responsibility for a certain area of the business, then that person should have the final say on the areas under his/her area of responsibility. If you, or a member of your staff, is responsible for a particular area, that person should have 51 percent of the vote in that area of responsibility. When you trust and empower your staff, productivity and profitability grow. Build a process for regular communication, and accept the fact that by surrendering oversight and implantation of certain activities, you will gain more control and greater impact on those areas in which you exercise your unique genius.

At the risk of sounding contradictory, you have the final responsibility for every aspect of the business—after all, it is your business. There will be times when you have to overrule a colleague, and you need to build those exceptions into your communication policy and procedures, and let your associates know in no uncertain terms when and why that could happen.

Questions & Action Steps

1. *What repetitive tasks do you and your TEAM engage in that should be codified in the form of a formal process?*

2. *Do you have regular letters or routine client correspondence that could be built into form letters to prevent the same letter from being drafted more than once?*

3. *What processes do you use that a checklist would simplify, and in doing so, enhance client service and protect you and your business from liability?*

4. *Do you have your telephone greeting scripted, making your communication consistent and making it easy to train new staff?*

chapter 6

Ultimate small CAP:
Education and Training

A good rule of thumb—either hire experienced people and pay them what they are worth, or hire inexperienced people with great potential and train them. If you choose people that need a lot of training, don't forget your primary role (in other words, don't quit selling) and focus all of your time on training. In addition, advisors sometimes forget their *personal* need for training and education. Advisors also benefit from designing a continuing education strategy for *themselves*, as well as for their staff. In order to build a training program that benefits the advisor and staff, it is often helpful for the advisor to construct an formal, well designed educational development plan for his/her team, as well as a personal educational plan.

One caveat—have a basic skill set requirement for anyone you hire and for each position for which you hire. In other words, these basic skills form the minimum skills required for employment. This set of skill requirements differs from a minimum *functional* educational requirement. For example, it makes no sense to hire someone who has met educational requirements but lacks basic office skills.

The training plan planning and development process contains four simple steps.

- Defining a training philosophy
- Building a training structure
- Constructing a training delivery schedule
- Execution and evolution

Defining a Training Philosophy

An advisor's training philosophy resembles a mission statement for the business's training department. An example of a training philosophy might include principles such as:

- Offer educational and training opportunities that help our associates successfully achieve their career objectives while assisting them in providing greater value to the business.

- Provide product and process knowledge and skills to better serve our clients.

- Help our associates develop their communication and selling skills used to serve our clients in a friendly and effective manner.

The training philosophy should help keep the advisor's teams focused on consistently improving all areas of the business—not just for the sake of efficiency but to be more effective by providing improved, personal client service, serving more clients, and growing revenues.

Building a Training Structure

Most people appreciate structure, and training programs are no exception. Consistency in the basic training structure helps professional staff know what they will receive and what is expected of them. Training structure might contain the following training segments.

- Product knowledge
- Communication skills
- Process training
- Cross-training

Product Knowledge Training

Different staff members require different levels of product knowledge. However, often it makes sense for the entire team to be familiar with the basics of what products do, how they work, and how to service them. Financial service product manufacturers and distributors provide numerous sales brochures, product guides, and

Web resources to provide the training core, as well as provide future-reference resources.

Communications Skills Training

Communication skills, or what is often referred to as people knowledge, complement product knowledge. The ability to effectively communicate with clients and lead them to action provides the real value in a financial advisory business. Financial product/service manufacturers offer products of all types on the Internet. The ability of the advisor and staff to develop deep relationships *and* provide technical competency often make the difference for consumers when they make the choice to buy products on the Web or from a trusted advisor. Technical competency remains essential for advisors and their teams, but they must be able to communicate. Examples of communications skills training include:

- Telephone training
- Basic selling skills
- Interviewing and questioning techniques
- Presentation skills

Many advisors seek this type of training individually, but neglect to offer training opportunities for their staffs. Professional staff often have more contact with clients than the advisor, so it is worth the investment of time and resources to train staff.

Process Training

Processes guide the execution of the advisor's business. Process training involves those routines of the business, including, but not limited to:

* Processing trades and applications
* Completing sales logs and blotters
* Marketing program implementation
* Client service implementation
* Seminar and event planning
* Telephone procedures
* Service call procedure
* Administration procedures

Including these processes in the Standard Operation Procedures Manual (SOPM) mentioned earlier helps the advisor develop routine that accelerates training, improves efficiency, and allows the advisor to focus on client sales.

Cross-Training

As advisors add staff, they should consider cross-training at every opportunity. Staff get sick, have personal emergencies, and leave for other jobs. Cross-training along with a SOPM ensures the advisor's office continues to operate smoothly and the advisor continues to function at a high level of efficiency and effectiveness when there are disruptions to staff. In addition, having staff cross-train on every process also helps them understand their colleagues' responsibilities. While the advisor does not need to understand every detail of the staff's execution of their responsibilities, he/she does need to understand basic processes to make certain they are appropriate for the advisor's office and within the regulatory guidelines of the supervising firm.

Who Pays For Training?

If an advisor offers ongoing training for professional staff, who pays for the training? Believe it or not, the answer to this question might not be so obvious. A suggested rule of thumb provides general guidance when addressing this question.

1. If the training is required to do the job, and the employee did not have the training prior to employment, the employer pays for the training. (If the advisor hires someone who can't do the job because the person doesn't have *basic* skills, no problem, *if* you plan on providing training for those skills.)

2. If the training helps the employee advance on his/her career path, the employee pays for the training.

These two simple guidelines can provide the basis for training cost participation. Mitigating circumstances might include the following considerations.

- Is there a hard cost (as in the case of sending a member of the staff to a for-fee seminar on telephone marketing) to the training? If the advisor is the person doing the training, there is no cost issue, but do consider the opportunity cost of the advisor exchanging sales time for training time.

- If there is a hard cost to the training, such as a seminar or workshop that would fall under guideline number two, it shows support and encouragement to pay a *portion* of the cost. If the employee wants the training, and it will help that person advance his/her career, or qualify for a better compensation package, but the person is not willing to pay a portion of the cost, that tells you that employee may not be committed to professional excellence.

- If the employee's portion is significant, have the employee sign a simple note and deduct the payments from his/her paycheck.

These types of exceptions or addendums to your training policy help make it easier for your team to enhance their skills and offer better service to your clients. Whenever you encourage your staff or associates to improve themselves, it helps you build your business, and it helps them prepare to grow with you.

What About Your Training?

This is a challenging business and the professional advisor must always look at how to improve his/her personal skill sets. The advisor's required skills parallel the needs of staff—the advisor just has more on the line. In addition, the advisor must be able to make recommendations *and* lead the prospect or client to a logical conclusion. With the amount of continuing education required to maintain financial product sales and service licensure, advisors allow their companies to map out the advisor's training plan. Taking charge of developing one's own personal training plan, based on the advisor's unique strengths and weaknesses, helps that advisor improve skill sets that create better qualitative and quantitative results. Simply put, with the right training, the advisor sees greater sales, improved client satisfaction, or a combination of both.

Hiring a Coach

Tiger Woods ranks among the greatest golfers of all time. Arguably, he may be the best individual performer in the world at *any* endeavor—but he still needs the advice of his caddy and a coach. When you are the best, why do you need a coach? A coach provides objective feedback questions to help an advisor accurately assess situations and opportunities and a measure of accountability. Consider hiring a coach to assist you in developing:

1. Better selling skills
2. Marketing guidance and strategy
3. Improved practice management

An advisor cannot maximize the value and quantity of his/her business without addressing the three critical performance areas of selling, marketing, and practice management. For free coaching tools and a questionnaire to determine if you are coach-able, go to www.michaelroby.com/usc/coaching.

Constructing a Training Delivery Schedule

All the plans in the world are of little value if not implemented. Now that you have developed a training philosophy, and built your structure, it is time to schedule training. Caution: don't train so often or so intensely that you overwhelm your TEAM, or yourself, for that matter. The best trainers never quit training, but sometimes the best learning is a result of letting a person experience a situation, and they process the information they gather from the experience. So how often is often enough to train?

Sales training for people new to selling is often scheduled weekly after an intensive boot camp training program. Boot camps often consist of daily training that last one to three weeks. Longer, more intensive training is often delivered by training departments at the home office or regional level. Basic sales training delivered on a local level can be delivered weekly during non-peak selling hours. Basic training involves telling and showing, so joint sales calls are frequently included as part of the program. Regular sales training works well when scheduled on a monthly basis, once again, during non-peak selling hours. As your team grows, ask colleagues to assist with training. Very often, the teacher learns the most. Training for staff can be as simple as a telephone technique or process training. Some training can be outsourced, as a number of high quality training programs are offered at the local level by training companies and community colleges.

Execution and Evolution

The last step is execution of your training program. You created a training schedule, so you'll want to follow the schedule. Do not operate in a vacuum, however. Be aware of what's going on with your TEAM and the training. You may want to deviate your schedule, but don't. The effect of some training can be seen almost immediately, but some training needs to be evaluated over a longer period of time. Adjust your training program to your needs and the needs of your associates. Measuring sales activity and call reports provides a picture of the effectiveness of training. For example, measuring closing ratios, contact ratios, and source of funds reports help you determine the needs of your TEAM.

Practice Management

Practice management means the difference between just selling and building a business. Many advisors (especially those in the business for a short period of time) say something similar to "I just want to sell and take care of my clients. I don't really want to run a business." However, if the advisor stays in the business for a couple of years, he/she starts to plateau at some point. Service work demands more time. A well planned sales day deteriorates to chasing one client's problem after another. A conversation with a client results in the advisor scratching his/her head because it's been *so long* since the last contact with the client. Then a client leaves for another advisor. Perplexed, the advisor had no idea this was happening. Exasperated, the advisor calls the (former) client and is shocked to find the client really was satisfied with the service rendered, but decided to move the account to another advisor anyway.

At this point, if you are saying, "Wow, that has happened to *me!*" you might just have a practice management problem. The solution calls for you to manage your practice as if you were managing a business for another person. Look at each area of your business, and ask yourself:

1. Am I running this area of my business *effectively*?

2. Am I running this area of my business *efficiently*?

The difference between effectiveness and efficiency is:

- Effectiveness is *doing the right things*.

- Efficiency is *doing things right*.

First, make certain you *are* doing the right things. This includes prospecting, selling, marketing, and the other areas that generate revenue, give clients good service, and help your business run smoothly. Second, examine those areas with an eye for completing the tasks that allow you to achieve these outcomes quicker and better. If you focus on efficiency first, you may develop a good process for doing something that has no significant impact on the success of your business. Do not major in minors.

When an advisor is comfortable that he/she *is* doing the right things, and it is showing up as good results, that advisor has reached the point when efficiency becomes important. This does not just happen; you must manage this process, and nobody can do this but you.

Administrative Staffing—Building a TEAM

As you build your business, you want assistants who can function in a team environment. If a particular role does not demand the need to function as part of a team, that position can be outsourced. Outsourcing provides additional opportunities for your business, in that resources of time and money can be focused on tasks that are specific to obtaining your sales objectives. If tasks are completed by an employee or outsourced, the people involved are still part of your TEAM. Every sales TEAM has four key attributes. These attributes provide a framework to help you help your staff grow your business. As discussed in chapter one, solid sales TEAM is:

T = Trained

E = Enthusiastic

A = Assistants who are

M = Managed by *you*

Let's discuss each of these factors in more detail.

Training

As mentioned earlier, every person you hire to be a part of your staff comes to you with a certain set of basic professional skills, such as the ability to meet people well, provide customer service focus, solve problems, understand process management, and execute basic office skills. However, the financial advisory industry demands that one also be able to adapt to an ever-changing business. *Every* business changes, but with the ever increasing product proliferation and rapid technological changes on top of the financial markets, change is accelerated and exacerbated past the ability of some people to adapt. Your staff must be able to adapt to change, and, if they are to adapt, they must be trainable. Serving clients who become frightened and anxious in mercurial markets is not easy, so clients must also be coachable. In spite of the fact that so much training can be outsourced, you will always have the role of part-time trainer, but you need to coach your staff almost daily to inspire them to provide the best in client service.

Enthusiastic

Being smart and well-trained is not enough; your staff needs to possess a spirit of enthusiasm and a heart to serve. They need to be able to execute process (don't forget compliance), but, at the same time, be flexible, intuitive, and willing to look for better solutions. This requires enthusiasm! How can an advisor build and maintain enthusiasm in his/her sales TEAM? Here are five tips that work.

1. Hire people who are naturally enthusiastic and passionate.
2. Reward success immediately.
3. Be consistent and flexible simultaneously.
4. Expect greatness.
5. Co-create a career path.

Let's briefly discuss each of these tips.

Hire People Who Are Naturally Enthusiastic And Passionate

People possess a basic nature, an internal basic programming language that affects and colors every aspect of how they view the world. The source and reasons for this programming are beyond the scope and purpose of this text. While I can't explain the source and causation of this programming, I do know this—people *can* change, but rarely *do they change*. If you hire someone who possesses a bad attitude but is well trained and educated, usually that person won't change, and you can't make him/her change. People will come to you from poisoned work environments and they can be a valuable addition to your staff, but if they have a less than positive attitude, usually the attitude will not change. Hire people that don't need to be repaired.

Reward Success Immediately

When a member of your team achieves a good outcome, tell that person immediately. Everyone likes a pat on the back. Some advisors feel they should not have to praise their employees. "They get paid to do the work," is the justification for not offering prompt praise. Don't miss an opportunity to reinforce good results; positively reinforced behaviors and activities will be repeated,

Be Consistent and Flexible Simultaneously

The financial advisory business demands discipline and consistency. Consistency with your staff provides a workplace environment that allows your TEAM to work with a reasonable expectation of the results of their efforts. For example, if you allow a member of your staff to attend a school function during the workday when the workload is covered, and then turn down a request for another employee in a similar situation, you set yourself up for sniping and the development of petty jealousies in your office. Inconsistent leadership isn't leadership, just poor management. Inconsistency causes employees to be anxious, and anxious employees can't put their focus on the client, so be consistent in your leadership. This may seem to be a paradox to consistency, but it is not a paradox if you are consistently flexible. In actuality, consistent flexibility is a policy that insures you are treating your staff as human beings, not just as employees. When work is caught up, it can be good business to let someone off early, especially when that team member has been putting in long hours on a marketing project, or endured a long day of challenging clients. Another example is an employee's request to look at a different way to manage an office process. Everything can be improved; consistent flexibility allows all things to be challenged and creates an atmosphere of continual improvement.

Expect Greatness

Too often we accept good performance, and then expect no more. *Expect greatness from every member of your staff.* Encourage them to expand their horizons through additional training or participating in an event or activity that is outside their comfort zone. Your confidence and expectation of greatness speaks volumes about your commitment to them, their potential, and your common future together.

Co-Create A Career Path

An assistant may or may not have aspirations of being an advisor. In fact, you may not wish to add advisors to your TEAM. However, no employee (like an advisor), ever "gets there." People can always do more, always grow, so discuss a career path with everyone on your staff at the time of hiring, and during every review. Establishing a career path for a staff member is not something that is done for them, but by encouraging your employees to grow and by guiding them to develop a personal career path, you help them transcend their present positions. This process helps them to look to the future, and people tend to work hard when marching towards their dreams.

Everyone would love to have a perfect world. However, while nothing is ever perfect, there is magic and power in trying to perfect something; this magic affects jobs as well. When hiring and during reviews, ask your employees the following question:

"How can we work together to make this the perfect job for you?"

This question creates a scenario where your employees see your personal interest in them as people, not just their job. You may be amazed by the topics that come up. This isn't a one-way conversation, however. This conversation becomes a type of negotiation. For example, if an employee wants some flexibility in work hours, this allows you to discuss an expansion of responsibilities. There is never something for nothing. Also, there will be requests that just cannot work, but the exercise of co-creating this perfect world will pay big dividends for your employee, you, and your clients.

These tips will work for you if you are genuinely interested in your staff as people. So make sure you know your employees personally. Spend time with them and their families outside of the business. A dinner, sporting event, or party helps add a personal element to professional relationships, and, if your employees see you as someone who is genuinely interested in them as people, they will run through walls for you. Make these off-site activities a part of your business plan, and you will see the results in improved productivity from a loyal and committed TEAM.

Enthusiasm makes a good business great! Fostering, recognizing, and rewarding enthusiasm allows advisors to continue to create and develop enthusiasm in their business.

Questions & Action Steps

1. *What areas of the business do you most need additional training and education? Have you developed an individualized training program for your TEAM members? How and when do you plan to provide that training?*

2. *Do you have a personal training calendar? In which areas of the business do you most need additional training and education? How and when do you plan to schedule and receive that training?*

chapter 7
Ultimate small CAP:
Potpourri

The basics of success as a financial advisor comprise a fairly short list. To be successful, an advisor must:

1. Tell the right story to a large number of people,
2. Make solid recommendations based on proven strategies,
3. Provide excellent service.

To go beyond success to excellence, the list becomes much longer. In this section, we will review some of the finishing touches that help you continue to move toward exceptional excellence.

Firing Clients

Early in an advisor's career there is no such thing as a bad client. Any business is good business, and your main focus is client acquisition. At some point, client service demands more time, and time devoted to sales goes down. To build profitability, account size becomes more important than the sheer numbers of clients— clients that have come to expect your door to always be open and you to always answer the phone within two rings. You notice you don't spend as much time with your largest and best clients, and referrals might go down. This time is precisely when your clients that can be a challenge start to consume a larger percentage of your time. These clients call frequently wanting to know "What's the market going to do this year/quarter/month/week/today?" Your judgment is called into question, and they ask you to reduce premiums and cut commissions, often comparing you to other advisors or online services. They never seem to be happy; you can't do enough. These problem clients consume an inordinate amount of time and drag you and your staff down whenever they come in or call on the phone.

At this point, advisors should consider firing clients. Don't allow this action to appear harsh; if clients are not happy with the quality of your service, you will do them a favor to rearrange their servicing arrangement. Firing a client does not necessarily mean sending the client to another B/D, advisor, or financial institution. It might mean their account will be serviced and /or managed by a member of your staff. However, sometimes everyone is served best when the client does leave for another advisor at another firm.

The process of firing a client requires the advisor to position the change as beneficial to the ***client*** because it ***is*** better for them, as well as for you. If a client no longer fits your personal sales model, that client detracts from the service delivered to your other clients. No matter how problematic the client has become, do everything possible to put the burden for the deterioration of the client/advisor relationship upon you. This reduces the possibility of the client speaking poorly of you in conversations with other prospects. Follow these steps to give yourself the best possible odds on maintaining a civil personal relationship after termination of the professional relationship.

1. Personally call the client to schedule the appointment. Tell the client that something had come up concerning the account, and you need to see him/her personally in your office to discuss the situation. If the client asks what the problem is, tell him/her you would rather discuss it in person.

2. Greet the client warmly when he/she arrives. Say you have been thinking, and for whatever reason, the client has not been happy with the way the account has been handled. Don't assign blame, don't blame the client, and don't accept blame.

3. State that as important as it is to you to have him/her as a client, it is more important that he/she be happy with the manner in which the account is serviced.

4. As a result, you have decided that it is in the *client's* best interest if someone besides you serviced the account. Mention another potential advisor the client may wish to use, or ask to whom he/she would want the account transferred. Have the paperwork ready. If the client is not, as a rule, problematic, state you have decided to assign the responsibility for account servicing to your best service assistant, and that going forward, this assistant will be the client's primary contact in your office.

5. Be prepared for the client to protest, saying that he/she want *you* to continue to service the account. If you would consider continuing the advisor/client relationship, outline the conditions required to do so, such as:

   a. You expect him/her to follow your recommendations. Your value in the relationship is based upon your experience, knowledge, and opinions.

   b. You provide good value for the fees you charge. As a result, you will not provide commission or fee reductions. You must assign value to your services.

    c. The client *must* agree to periodic reviews.

    d. Other conditions of engagement as you see fit.

6. If the client is to transfer the account(s), you or your assistant should complete the process professionally and courteously.

When you fire a client, this frees your time and reduces your (and your staff's) stress. The client should do business elsewhere if he/she is not happy with the quality of your service. The odds are that nobody can make a difficult client happy, and it is not the obligation of the advisor to please everybody.

This strategy also works with bank advisors, who frequently call upon multiple branches and have high numbers of smaller accounts. Bank reps protest that "I *must* accept all accounts; after all, I work in a bank." Not true; loan officers turn down loans and other accounts that do not meet their standards. Financial advisors are no different. Other advisors squirm when asked to consider firing clients. Acquiring business is tough, and you hate to give up on a client, but, once again, you can't please everybody, and the energy drain caused by challenging clients is usually not worth the income generated.

Activity Management

New advisors absolutely need to set activity goals and track activity. Selling, as a business, provides its own method to keep score—tracking sales. Activity tracking and management also acts as a scoreboard—one that provides daily feedback. Activity numbers provide a methodology for analyzing sales skills as well. For example, if a salesperson has an adequate number of sales calls, but sales are not what they should be, there is either a quality prospect problem, presentation problem, or closing problem. Many lessons flow from sales activity analysis. Weekly statistics tracked might include:

* Contacts
* Calls
* Appointments
* Closing interviews
* Sales
* Average gross dealer concession (GDC) or commission per sale
* New assets under management (AUM)
* New referred leads

Experienced advisors also benefit from activity analysis. Much can be learned about the success of specific marketing campaigns, as well as the effectiveness of assistants who sell over the phone or in the office. The metrics used by experienced advisors differ from those used by newer advisors. While newer advisors concern themselves with basic activity, experienced advisors will look at statistics such as:

- Average GDC or commission per new account
- Revenue generated per hour
- New referrals/client contact
- New/New net AUM

Marketing initiatives require significant investment of hard dollars as well as the investment of time for the advisor and staff. Activity analysis lends itself to evaluating seminar marketing activities and the scheduling of client reviews. The advisor's time and resources devoted to training staff are maximized by knowing those areas that require the most attention for the TEAM. Tracking these activities for profitability and making adjustments allow the advisor and the staff to continually upgrade their marketing. On a quarterly or semi-annual basis, the advisor should look at sales results and determine the source of the sale. Tracking this data is very simple; all the advisor must do is add a field to the CRM program for source, (assuming this is not being tracked already). Statistics that help determine the effectiveness of your marketing include:

- Client Acquisition Cost (Total marketing program cost/Number of new clients)
- Revenue Acquisition Cost (GDC generated by a specific marketing program)

After determining these ratios, replace unprofitable or less profitable marketing programs with new ideas to continually improve your business. A word of caution—

do not be whip-sawed into changing marketing programs prematurely. Some marketing programs need more time to determine profitability. In addition, some marketing programs are intended to be passive marketing, such as newsletters and advertising.

Advertising

Some advisors (usually newer advisors) expect advertising to provide a significant boost to sales in and of itself. Rarely (if ever) does advertising drive sales in the financial services industry. Advertising drives sales in commodity businesses, or in businesses that offer products that people *buy*. Financial services must be *sold*. However, that does not mean you should not advertise. Financial advisors should advertise to:

1. Achieve name brand recognition

2. Promote yield

3. Promote seminars and other public selling events

Name brand recognition helps make the following statement work for a financial advisor:

"When prospects think of X, they think of me." (Where X defines the benefit you bring to prospects in the marketplace.) In other words, when you are walking down the street in your community, and a person asks someone else "Who is that?" a large percentage of people actually know what you do. That is name brand recognition.

Yield advertising provides value for the advisor that has a particular investment that provides an attractive rate of income stream. Many times yield products provide relatively low GDC, but advisors advertise yield products to generate new relationships. Yield advertising generates traffic.

For marketing seminars or other public selling events, event advertising provides a profitable use of advertising dollars. While attendance is the primary objective, an ancillary benefit is name brand recognition. Non-attendees may notice the advisor's event and activity within the marketplace.

One last point on advertising: Use your picture in all of your ads. Let people see you are a real person. When prospective clients recognize you, a sales barrier is removed because the prospect knows who you are and what you do.

Resources and Relationships

Successful advisors utilize a variety of resources to compress time and accelerate their business growth. Careful consideration of these resources adds greatly to the probability of success for newer advisors, as well as the rate of growth for seasoned advisors. Making a dynamic list of resources allows the advisor to maximize the value of his/her business. Keeping the list dynamic is critical. Some advisors become emotionally attached to products, product providers, strategies, and ideas after their time has passed. The two guiding principles in decisions related to resources and relationships include:

First, "Is this decision/relationship in the client's best interest?"

Second, "Will this decision/relationship help me grow my business?"

Some important resources and relationships include:

- Your Broker/Dealer
- Insurance companies
- Investment companies
- Compliance services
- Wholesalers
- Sales, marketing, or other business coaches

Your Broker/Dealer

Broker/Dealers (B/Ds) provide services to the advisor in return for a portion of GDC. Take an objective look at your B/D and the services you receive from them. These services include business processing, client statements, product due-diligence, training, sales conferences, networking with other registered reps of the firm, commission accounting, compliance services (more on compliance later), and more. How can these services help you grow your business? Examine each of these services for their business-building capabilities, and make certain you are taking full advantage of these services.

Insurance Companies

Insurance companies offer much more than product. Advanced underwriting, income planning, and financial planning services provide real value to you and your clients. Continuing education offered by insurers helps you maintain the licensure needed to maintain your business, and sales desks provide sales and service ideas to help you grow that business. Are you using these services for maximum advantage for your clients and your business?

Investment Companies

Investment companies, which for this discussion include mutual funds, separately managed funds, unit trusts, real estate investment trusts, limited partnerships, and others, provide many of the same services. In addition, they provide statistical information and data on their product genre as well as broad market history and trends. Comparisons to other asset classes, asset allocation studies, and services add to the value provided by these firms. What information do you need to help you grow your business by helping your clients?

Compliance Services

Your B/D's compliance department provides primary source of your compliance oversight, but consider how compliance and due-diligence act as additional resources that protect your clients. For example, asset allocation models and product allocation provide the advisor with guidelines for prudent portfolio selection and risk management. Suitability is everyone's business; your compliance department offers an additional set of eyes to protect you and your client. The compliance department is *not* the sales prevention department, but a firewall to help you keep your business legal and your clients protected. Work at understanding the rationale behind the guidelines to become a better marketer and better advisor.

Wholesalers

While insurance companies, investment companies, and other product providers usually distribute their products with a wholesale field force, their services vary by company. Many industry professionals overuse the term "product partner," but when utilized correctly, professional wholesalers provide a host of tremendously valuable services for the financial advisor. Seminars, joint sales calls, training, sales ideas, and marketing support are but a few of the aspects of professional wholesaler support. When it comes to product, wholesalers demonstrate:

- The benefit received by the client if he/she uses the wholesaler's product,
- How the product works,
- Where the product fits, and
- How to sell the product.

Some of the ways wholesalers achieve these outcomes include:

- Sales ideas
- Marketing ideas
- Seminars
- Joint sales calls
- Marketing support
- Business planning assistance
- Training for you and for your team
- Marketing support

A term that wholesalers overuse is value added. Value added constitutes anything over and above product description that a wholesaler does that provides the advisor with the following benefits:

1. Grow your business
2. Streamline your business
3. Expand your product offerings
4. Improve client service

Wholesalers provide advisors with a wealth of resources. Properly utilized, these resources can be a business asset that can help you achieve the four benefits of value added. Unfortunately, some advisors take advantage of wholesalers with no intent of a valid business purpose. Instead, they see wholesalers as an unlimited source of dinners, golf games, and event tickets. Obviously, there are better ways to interface with wholesalers for your best business advantage. When you consider product partners, consider the following criteria:

- Quality of the company and its management,
- Quality of their products,
- Do their products fit your business?
- The ability of the wholesaler to be a resource that will help you utilize the products and help you grow your business.

An excellent strategy is to prepare a short joint marketing plan with your primary product wholesalers. Agree what each of you will do to add to the relationship. Make a contract with each other and commit to helping each other. Adding strategy to these relationships helps both parties by providing plans and tactics to increase sales and better serve clients.

A word about wholesaler loyalty is in order. Never sell a product because you are loyal to a wholesaler. Sell the product, if and only if, the product solves a problem and provides a solution for your client. If more than one company offers a particular solution for a client need, all things being equal, sell the product from the company whose wholesaler and whose personal services provide the greatest value, and with whom you have the best relationship. The bottom line is this: sell the product that does the best job of solving your client's problem *and* helps you grow your business.

Questions & Action Steps

1. *What resources can I utilize to help me build my business?*

2. *How can I better partner with my broker/dealer and financial product providers to grow my business and better serve my clients?*

3. *Am I doing all I can do to meet compliance rules and regulations, and how can I use compliance to protect my clients and myself?*

4. *Which wholesalers not only represent quality companies, but also provide additional services to help me grow my business?*

5. *How can I best utilize wholesaler services, seminars, joint sales calls, competitive analysis, marketing support? How much business will I need to send to them to be able to expect this support?*

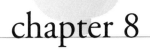

chapter 8

Ultimate small CAP:
Where Do You Go From Here?

Within these pages are numerous strategies, tactics, and tips about how to build and grow a financial advisory practice. Within this information a common thread exists—first and foremost:

The needs of the client *always* come first!

Regardless of your distribution channel, this is the keystone upon which the entire industry is built. Your objective is to build a business or a practice that will allow you to reach your personal and professional goals, but that goal is without meaning in the absence of a client that is well served. It matters not that you are an independent planner, wirehouse broker, bank advisor, or an insurance agent—*you must take care of the client's needs first!*

Should you come to feel that your distribution partner does not have the client's best interests at heart, you should consider aligning yourself with a firm that recognizes the sacred trust associated with the direct or implied fiduciary relationship you have with your prospects and companies. All business decisions take a back seat to the needs of the people you seek to serve.

Second, to maximize the value you bring to the marketplace and your compensation for that value, crystallize your vision of what you want your business to look like one, two, five, and ten years in the future. Within your vision, consider questions such as:

- How many clients do I wish to serve?

- How much income do I want to generate?

- What type of wealth do I want to build? (There is a big difference between income and wealth.)

- How will I deliver my services?

- How will I help my team grow and reach their objectives?

Build a business plan to make that vision become reality. (See chapter four). Address all of the activities needed to make your vision a reality. Consider various contingencies should (due to circumstances beyond your control) your plans not go as expected. Then get to work and make your dreams and the dreams you have for your family come true.

A Word About Balance

There is no business or business goal that would be worth the sacrifice of your health, family, and friends. Make certain you achieve your personal and family goals by devoting the same stringent planning to your personal activities as you do for your business. Plan your family activities in your plan next to your business goals. You can have it all; you just can't do it all on the same day. Review this part of your plan with your "Family Board of Directors." Your business goals are the means to the end of your personal and family goals.

Commit To Excellence in Everything You Do

Take this book and use it as a guideline, a path, if you will, to help you become the best advisor you can be for your clients, your company, your family, and yourself. Not all of the ideas in this book will be of benefit to you as you seek to grow your business. Take what you like and leave the rest. Commit to excellence in everything you do as you seek to build

The Ultimate Small Cap Business

YOURS!

TO DO section

In this section, write down any ideas you wish to explore
further or implement in your business.

_____

_____

_____

_____

_____

_____

_____

_____

_____

_____

_____

_____

glossary of terms

Assets Under Management (AUM)—Client assets for which the financial advisor has custody, control, fiduciary responsibility, or service responsibility.

Broker/Dealer (B/D)—Any individual or firm in the business of buying and selling securities for itself and others. Broker/dealers must register with the SEC. When acting as a broker, a broker/dealer executes orders on behalf of his/her client. When acting as a dealer, a broker/dealer executes trades for his/her firm's own account. If a financial advisor sells registered securities, he/she is a Registered Representative of that B/D.

Distribution Channel—A financial advisor's delivery system. Distribution Channels include:

> **Bank Advisor**—Financial advisors housed in a financial institution, such as a bank or credit union. May be employees or registered reps of a third party marketer.

> **Captive Agency**—Advisors that are insurance agents working exclusively for a single company.

> **Independent Advisor**—Non-employee Registered Reps that sell securities and (at some level) guide clients on life insurance, pensions, funds, and other financial product decisions.

> **Independent Agency**—Insurance agents that provide insurance (and other financial products) to clients from several companies.

> **Regional Brokerage House**—A brokerage firm of 800+ Registered Representatives traditionally associated with stock brokerage.

> **Wirehouse**—A brokerage firm of 800+ Registered Representatives traditionally associated with stock brokerage.

Financial Industry Regulatory Authority (FINRA)—The largest non-governmental regulator for all securities firms doing business in the United States. FINRA oversees nearly 5,100 brokerage firms, about 174,000 branch offices, and more than 672,000 registered securities representatives. Founded in July 2007, through the consolidation of NASD and the member regulation, enforcement, and arbitration functions of the New York Stock Exchange.

Gross Dealer Concessions (GDC)—Gross Dealer Concessions include fees, commissions, and any other income derived from sales of financial products and services.

Multiple Advisor Practice (MAP)—A business with more than one advisor, which is owned or managed by a principal advisor/manager/general agent.

Registered Representative—An individual who is licensed to sell securities and has the legal power of an agent, having passed the Series 7 and Series 63 examinations. Usually works for a brokerage licensed by the SEC, NYSE, and FINRA.

Single Advisor Practice (SAP)—A sole practitioner that does not have, or plan to add, additional advisors to his/her business.

Standard Operating Procedures Manual (SOPM)— A manual created by an advisor that contains process and procedures that are used to run the business and guide and train staff members.

Wholesaler—A company representative that is responsible for distributing financial products through financial advisors or intermediaries.

Michael Roby is a sales and marketing strategist, author, and professional speaker. In thirty years in the financial services industry, Mike has continually demonstrated excellence and leadership as a financial advisor, sales manager, and investment wholesaler. As an authority on financial product distribution and marketing, he is a sought after speaker and trainer by banks, broker/dealers, money managers, and insurance companies. In addition, Mike writes a regular marketing column for *Bank Advisor Magazine*. Mike is a professional member of the National Speakers Association (NSA) and NSA-Minnesota, serving NSA-Minnesota as a director and member of the executive committee. In addition, Mike has been named "Member of the Year" by NSA-Minnesota. Mike and his wife, Melanie, live in Savage, Minnesota.